Symbols of Power & Progress

American Trademarks 1930 to 1950

Volume 2

Symbols of Power & Progress

American Trademarks 1930 to 1950

Volume 2

John Mendenhall

Second Printing 1993

ISBN: 0-88108-037-3 (cloth)
ISBN: 0-88108-112-4 (paper)

LCCC: 86-081966

Printed in the United States of America

Published by
Art Direction Book Company
10 East 39th Street
New York, N.Y. 10016

Typeset by Magee Typesetting, San Luis Obispo, California

For Kveta

Preface

I have had this feeling for the past few years that the evolution of trademark design has reached a momentary plateau. Along with the ever-increasing number of graphic designers that our schools are producing, there are burgeoning numbers of new corporations that are vying for unique solutions to identification problems. Meanwhile, our ubiquitous design annuals display their selections of the year's best, and doesn't it all seem so familiar?

With the simple abstract symbol, terse and austere, sometimes almost painful in its economy of form, one questions whether its audience, the non-designer, can find meaning in so many subtle variations and articulations of square, circle and triangle.

On the other hand, with the pictorial symbol, the non-designer is able to identify it as a *thing* that is, more or less, familiar. This *thing* has a name, and it can be described. For example, *Piggly Wiggly* (pig), or *TVA* (hand with lightning bolt). It is much more difficult a task for the non-designer to describe an abstract symbol because he lacks the highly specialized vocabulary required to do so. Therefore, between the abstract and the pictorial, the non-designer usually finds rapport with the latter.

In my twenty years as a graphic designer, trying to communicate visual ideas to client and general public alike, I have noticed that not only do people respond more to pictures than to shapes, but, more precisely, to pictures of human beings rather than to either animals or objects.

Of the trademarks presented in this volume, almost all are pictorial. So, am I advocating a return to what you see on these pages? Not exactly.

For all their humor and enthusiasm, these trademarks are exactly what they appear to be: naive and out of touch with *our* time. When these trademarks were designed, the U.S. was primarily a product based economy. But now we are more of a service based economy, and how does one symbolize venture capital, or software design, or genetic engineering? Also, there are more businesses now, and many of them are operating on a global scale, which raises the question of whether there are enough pictorial symbols to go around.

In navigation there is a technique called "Dead Reckoning", which enables a pilot or a captain, when lost in a fog, to determine his position by referring to records of the course and distances covered. With the aid of this very valuable documentation the navigator is able to accurately plot the location of his ship and calculate a new course and speed.

Books such as this one should perhaps be thought of as part of Graphic Design's record of course and distances covered. Now—who would like to be the navigator?

Michael Manwaring
June 18, 1986.

Acknowledgements

I would like to acknowledge and express sincere gratitude to the following individuals. Their assistance in the preparation of this book is most gratefully appreciated.

Brian Slagle, for helping in the task of retouching some of the marks. Diane Beaudet, who most graciously assisted in the typesetting and paste-up. Dan and Susan Piel, who edited the Introduction. The United States Trademark Office, for making their extensive collection available. And all of my students and friends, who gave so much encouragement and support during the realization of this project.

A special thanks to Michael Manwaring, who wrote the Preface to this volume.

An advertising illustration from *Time* magazine, 1930.

Introduction

"The Machine is at work moulding as well as destroying human character."
—Frank Lloyd Wright, 1932

Mr. Televox, a product of Westinghouse Laboratories, was used by the New York Edison Company to operate an electrical distribution station. When whistled to over the phone, he would break circuits and move levers. Illustration by W.T. Murch.

The 1930s was the decade in American history when the machine became a pervasive fixture in our domestic environment. In 1929 there were only 500,000 mechanical refrigerators in household use; through the subsequent ten years this number soared into the millions. Industrial designers such as Norman Bel Geddes and Raymond Loewy promoted the purchase of household appliances as one method of injecting renewed vitality into the Depression era economy. The more products purchased, as the reasoning went, the more workers would be required to man the factories. And as these workers increased their earning power, they would buy additional goods to replace the less sophisticated, obsolete products of the 1920s.

Industrial designers convinced businessmen of the importance of producing new, up-to-date consumer goods which would appeal to a more demanding public. The bulky and mechanically awkward appliances commonly found on store shelves before 1930 were consistently replaced by sleeker, streamlined designs emanating from the newly formed industrial design offices across the country.

The advertising industry was forced to change to meet the needs of selling these modern redesigns to a cost conscious consumer. The old methods of advertising, using cluttered typographic arrangements with ornate illustrations, were abandoned in favor of simpler layouts and bolder, starker images. Stodgy serif typefaces were suddenly out of fashion, replaced by a preference for the sleeker forms of script or sans serif designs. One German typeface design in particular, the machine-inspired Futura, was the typographic equivalent of the new product design. Its clean geometry excised all ornament; outmoded serifs were stripped away to allow each engineered letterform to stand on its own simplicity. Even the name of this typeface suggests the timely break from past typographic traditions.

The intricate pen and ink drawings which were commonplace in advertising since its inception no longer seemed in touch with the times. To sell the

An exercise in constructive spatial design by Chernikhov, from a series on machine architecture.

streamlined designs of the 1930s required the same expression in graphic form. High contrast visuals with strong shadows, silhouettes and human forms composed from geometric shapes were the fashion.

Americans did not invent this approach to image-making. Following the October 1917 Revolution, Russian avant-garde artists experimented with the construction of images using basic, geometric forms. Iakov Chernikov created bold designs of abstracted machinery constructed from smooth planes. His philosophy of utilizing technology as an inspiration in visual image-making is evident throughout his 1931 book, *The Construction of Architectural and Machine Forms:* "Far from lying beyond the boundaries of our aesthetic understanding, machinery possesses aesthetic norms and canons of its own which are entirely cogent and unquestionable."

Chernikov was one voice in many who heralded the new rational approach to design which later came to be known as the Modern Movement. Acknowledging that advances in industrial production have created new needs and new habits, he emphasized: "One of the most powerful forces of our era is the imperative to organize things rationally, to justify things functionally..."

Two art movements which gained widespread popularity in the 1920s, Cubism and Precisionism, had a great influence on American illustrators and advertising designers. Precisionism in particular, with its austere, geometrically concise compositions, suggested the perfection of machine technology. Its flatness and simplicity of composition was well-suited to the need of advertising to make a bold, emphatic visual statement.

Karl Schulpig, 1922. Wholesale steel trademark.

In Germany, graphic designers such as Karl Schulpig and Lucien Bernhard were creating posters and trademarks of impeccable precision. By 1930 their work, along with that of other designers, was building on the principles of modernism as developed at the Bauhaus. Angularity and an absence of all ornament were indicative of German architecture and design. These qualities, which totally rejected the emotive, resulted in a severity of form which was never fully embraced by American designers in the 1930s.

For the most part, American design of this decade tends to be more humanistic than its German and Russian counterparts. Cultural differences, as well as the humbling experiences of the Great Depression are undoubtedly major factors in this distinction. The cool perfection of German design throughout the 1930s is almost intimidating. American design, in contrast, expresses a more primitive exhuberance. Accepting the advance of technology, many American designers such as Frank Lloyd Wright were still skeptical of it. Optimistic about the future, the country was not necessarily anxious to forego the human values which the machine threatened to displace.

The trademarks created for industries during this tumultuous era reflect this ambivalence. While capturing the spirit of progress and renewed prosperity, they often do so with a wit and naivety which is seemingly the antithesis of a mechanized society. The breadth of imagery used to convey a company or product's identity reflect the diversity of a nation.

Symbolic analogy was often used to communicate a mood of self-assurance. A pictorial design utilizing a muscleman, for instance, may represent a heavy industry. Yet the way that he is depicted is more tongue-in-cheek than intimidating. Fantasy figures, such as Reddy Kilowatt or a tomato with a top hat and monocle, humanize otherwise nondescript industries. And they do it with a self-deprecating humor which is virtually nonexistent in contemporary corporate identity.

Why are the trademarks of the 1930s and 1940s so different from those being produced today? Perhaps it was the spirit of the times which had not yet been submerged by the giant, impersonal conglomerates of the 1980s. Another reason may be that trademark designers of the past had more training in drawing and representational skills, and less in the manipulation of abstract form. They were adept at creating images that had content and conveyed a message. Today's designers are less concerned with substance. The content of modern trademarks is usually reduced to the vague connotations made by simple shapes. Being more concerned with providing a pleasing visual configuration than in communicating an idea, they tend to

A 1930s hotel advertisement.

be devoid of any emotive quality.

The more important reason for this difference in design is the nature of American business. Today's corporations are not prone to take chances. The banality of most contemporary trademarks is appealing to businessmen by virture of the fact that it is the status quo; safe, "modern," and noncontroversial. Would any company today be so daring as to use a nude woman to represent itself as did Bulova Watch in 1947? Could a nude be used in *any* American trademark now without being subjected to condemnation or censorship?

As graphic designers rushed to embrace what came to be known as Swiss design in the 1970s, that which was quirky or offbeat was dropped in favor of a rational, and subsequently more mundane approach to visual problem-solving. Not that the profession was entirely at fault; companies hoping to sell to the widest possible market demanded middle-of-the-road graphic design. Much the same situation exists today. Few major corporations would be so bold as Munsingwear was in 1939, when it adopted a symbol of three men standing in underwear as its corporate identity! Yet this mark still communicates meaning more precisely than any current abstract form could.

The designs in the two volumes of this collection are not only inventive, but in many respects daring for the period in history in which they were created. Musclemen, mythological figures, cartoon characters, machine parts, eagles and assorted other animals were all incorporated into the symbols of the 1930s. Their personality is still clearly evident today.

As visual images these trademarks continue to be warm, friendly and accessible. They can be criticized in some instances for being too cute or simplistic; rarely are they boring. A good part of their charm is that they have not been pushed and modelled to perfection, but rather stand as emphatic, spirited statements of America's dreams and desires. Though molded by the Machine, these symbols communicate with an eloquence that is unmistakenly human.

Advertising throughout the 1930s often featured nude or partially clothed men and women. A 1935 advertisement for the Medusa Portland Cement Company.

Bibliography

A Treasury of German Trademarks
Leslie Cabarga
Art Direction: New York, 1982

American Epoch
Arthur S. Link
Alfred A. Knopf: New York, 1973

Fantasy and Construction
Iakov Chernikhov
Architectural Design Profile: London, 1984

Images of America
Karen Tsujimoto
University of Washington Press: Seattle, 1982

Men and Machines
Stuart Chase
The MacMillan Company: New York, 1929

Illustration by W.T. Murch
from *Men and Machines*, by
Stuart Chase, 1929.

Ford Motor Company
Dearborn, Michigan
Mercury 8 Service Mark, 1940

The Firestone Tire & Rubber Company
Akron, Ohio
Air Conditioning Units, 1940

Big Jack Manufacturing Company
Bristol, Virginia
Men's Work Clothing, 1943

Will Ross, Incorporated
Milwaukee, Wisconsin
Surgical Equipment, 1934

National Exposition of Power
and Mechanical Engineering
New York, New York
Service Mark, 1946

Schumacher Wall Board Corporation
South Gate, California
Gypsum Wall Board, c. 1939

Sturdee Storage Battery Company
Philadelphia, Pennsylvania
Storage Batteries, 1947

Titanium Pigment Company
New York, New York
Pigments Used in Rubber, 1933

Gershon & Schreiber
New York, New York
Bindings, 1934

I.F. Laucks, Incorporated
Seattle, Washington
Glue, 1936

Geneva Forge, Incorporated
Geneva, New York
Cutlery, 1934

Henry Joseph
Brooklyn, New York
Adhesive Cements, 1940

Consolidated Sewing Machine Company
New York, New York
Belts for Machinery, 1934

Wembley, Incorporated
New Orleans, Louisiana
Men's Neckties, 1939

Hercules Powder Company
Wilmington, Delaware
Cellulose, 1938

Samson Cordage Works
Boston, Massachusetts
Braided Cotton Cord, c. 1935

Medusa Portland Cement Company
Cleveland, Ohio
Cement, 1935

Mars Signal-Light Company
Chicago, Illinois
Signal Lamps, 1947

Wilson Sporting Goods Company
Chicago, Illinois
Golf Equipment, c.1940

The Celotex Corporation
Chicago, Illinios
Ceiling Tiles, c.1936

The Thalhammer Corporation
Los Angeles, California
Cameras and Tripods, 1930

The Pep Boys
Philadelphia, Pennsylvania
Lubricating Oils, 1933

Prest-O-Lite Storage Battery Corporation
Indianapolis, Indiana
Storage Batteries, 1937

F.S. Brainard & Company
Hartford, Connecticut
Rate Recorders for Water Meters, 1938

Archer's Hair Grower
Borger, Texas
Hair Grower, 1936

William Schield Manufacturing Company
St. Louis, Missouri
Pharmaceuticals, c. 1930

John Sunshine Chemical Company
Chicago, Illinois
Drain Pipe Cleaner, 1938

The Kroger Grocery Company
Cincinnati, Ohio
Spices, 1931

The Harrison Paint & Varnish Corporation
Canton, Ohio
Asbestos Roof Paint, 1937

Dovre Ski Binding Company
West Concord, Massachuetts
Ski Bindings, 1936

Witchell-Sheill Company
Chicago, Illinois
Athletic Shoes, 1934

RCA Service Company
Camden, New Jersey
Theater Sound Equipment Repair, 1949

Ruger Equipment Company
Uhrichsville, Ohio
Portable Hydraulic Floor Cranes, 1946

Boit, Dalton & Church Incorporated
Boston, Masschusetts
Insurance, 1946

Lockwood, Kessler and Bartlet
Brooklyn, New York
Engineers and Surveyors, c. 1930

Lily-Tulip Cup Corporation
New York, New York
Paper Cups, 1940

Baldwin Dairies, Incorporated
Philadelphia, Pennsylvania
Milk and Cream, 1946

Hot Shoppes, Incorporated
Washington D.C.
Restaurants, 1940

Richardson Corporation
Rochester, New York
Toppings Used for Making Sundaes, 1941

Puritan Chemical Company
Atlanta, Georgia
Cleaning Products, 1942

Provident Trust Company
Philadelphia, Pennsylvania
Banking Services, 1948

Old Colony Paint & Chemical Company
Los Angeles, California
Paint Remover, 1938

The Quaker Oats Company
Chicago, Illinois
Furan Chemicals, 1948

Cowcream Specialty Shops
Denver, Colorado
Malted Milk, 1930

D'Arrigo Brothers Company
San Jose, California
Celery, 1942

Columbia Breweries, Incorporated
Tacoma, Washington
Beer, 1949

The Band Box Corporation
St. Louis, Missouri
Dry Cleaning Machinery, 1935

Nashawena Mills
New Bedford, Massachusetts
Textile Fabrics, 1936

Twin Couple Company
Poughkeepsie, New York
Radio Reception Elements, 1930

Edward Weck & Son
Brooklyn, New York
Surgical Cutting Instruments, 1930

Engineering Manufacturing Company
Sheboygan, Wisconsin
Drafting Equipment, 1937

Fink-Roselieve Company
New York, New York
Photographic Apparatus, 1936

The Meriden Gravure Company
Meriden, Connecticut
Printing, 1947

Henry Dravneek Incorporated
New York, New York
Fashion Photography, c.1949

Walgreen Company
Chicago, Illinois
Talcum and Face Powder, 1935

Universal Chemical Company
Camden, New Jersey
Fluid for Lighters, 1936

The Forest City Rubber Company
Cleveland, Ohio
Antiseptic Solution, 1935

Safeguard, Incorporated
New York, New York
Cutley, 1935

The White King Company
Los Angeles, California
Laundry Detergent, c.1930

Rotary Seal Company
Chicago, Illinois
Seals for Compressors, 1939

Stephano Brothers
Philadelphia, Pennsylvania
Smoking Tobacco, 1940

Automatic Alarms, Incorporated
Youngstown, Ohio
Burglar Alarms, c.1944

Julius Schmid, Incorporated
New York, New York
Prophylactics, 1939

M.H. Rhodes, Incorporated
Hartford, Connecticut
Electric Time Switches, 1931

Israel Bloom
New York, New York
Device for Carrying Gloves, 1940

The Garlock Packing Company
Palmyra, New York
Gaskets, c.1932

Meat Industry Suppliers, Incorporated
Chicago, Illinois
Curing Compounds, 1941

The Lander Company
New York, New York
Eyebrow and Eyelash Grower, 1935

Champion Container Company
Philadelphia, Pennsylvania
Paper Containers, 1935

The Cream of Wheat Corporation
Minneapolis, Minnesota
Breakfast Food, 1939

American Stove Company
St. Louis, Missouri
Domestic Gas Ranges, 1939

Poster Products, Incorporated
Chicago, Illinois
Advertising, 1935

Spaulding-Moss Company
Boston, Massachusetts
Blue Print Paper, 1937

The Brunswick-Balke-Collender Company
Chicago, Illinois
Score Sheets, 1944

Geigy Company
New York, New York
Moth-Proofing Chemicals, 1940

C.G. Conn Ltd.
Elkhart, Indiana
Musical Instruments, 1933

Winter Brothers Company
Wrentham, Massachuetts
Taps and Dies, 1946

Ever Ready Label Corporation
New York, New York
Label and Gummed Tape, 1935

Munsingwear, Incorporated
Minneapolis, Minnesota
Men's and Boys' Underwear, 1939

Pendleton Detectives
New Orleans, Louisiana
Private Investigations, 1947

Philip Florin, Incorporated
New York, New York
Wallets, 1940

California Spray-Chemical Company
Berkeley, California
Ortho Service Mark, 1930

J.H. Thorp & Company
New York, New York
Upholstery and Drapery Fabrics, c.1944

Cortland Line Company
Cortland, New York
Fishing Lines, 1936

The Cleveland Paper Manufacturing Company
Cleveland, Ohio
Printing Papers, c.1930

Industrial Chemical Cleaner Company
Houston, Texas
Cleaning Compounds, 1947

Eagle-Ottawa Leather Company
Chicago, Illinois
Leather, 1937

Blackhawk Manufacturing Company
Milwaukee, Wisconsin
Hydraulic Jacks, 1937

Red Jacket Manufacturing Company
Davenport, Iowa
Water Systems, 1940

Harris Hardware & Manufacturing Company
New York, New York
Children's Bicycles, 1947

Mohican Pencil Company
Philadelphia, Pennsylvania
Pencils, 1933

Hickory Grove Coal Mining Corporation
Rochester, New York
Coal, 1938

Gamble-Skogmo, Incorporated
Minneapolis, Minnesota
Fishing Rods and Line, 1947

National Vulcanized Fibre Company
Wilmington, Delaware
Laminated Plastic, c.1935

Wilbur-Suchard Chocolate Company
Litiz, Pennsylvania
Chocolate, 1935

Howard D. Johnson Company
Quincy, Massachusetts
Fountain Syrups, 1949

Spalding Sales Corporation
Chicopee, Massachusetts
Golf Clubs, 1940

American Youth Hostels
1934

The Fair
Chicago, Illinois
Cleansing Tissue, 1931

Ault-Williamson Shoe Company
Auburn, Maine
Leather Shoes, 1936

United Coffee Corporation
San Francisco, California
Coffee, 1937

Jordon Marsh Company
Boston, Massachusetts
Women's Shoes, 1937

Hesperian Orchards
Wenatchee, Washington
Fresh Fruits, 1939

Emile Bernat & Sons Company
Jamaica Plain, Massachusetts
Yarn, 1934

Lanvin-Parfums, Incorporated
New York, New York
Perfumes, 1948

Brownberry Ovens, Incorporated
Oconomowoc, Wisconsin
Bakery Goods, 1950

Food Machinery Corporation
Riverside, California
"Miss Flavorseal"
Fruit Treatment, 1942

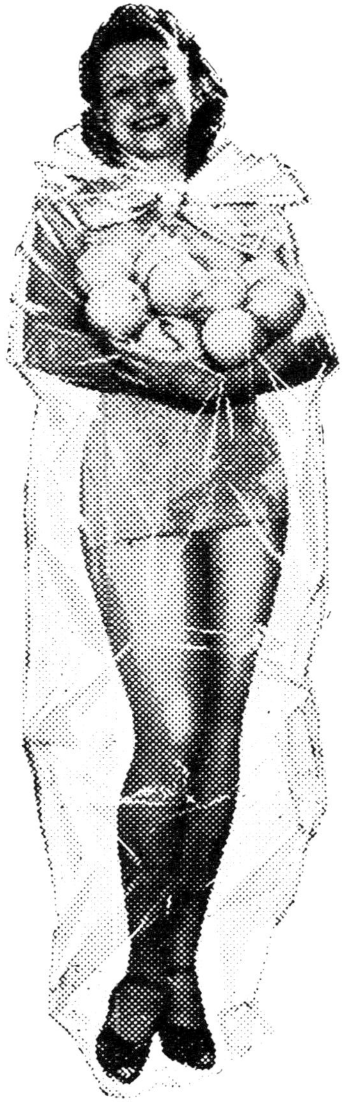

Chicago Board of Trade
Chicago, Illinois
"Ceres, Goddess of Grain"
Grain Market, 1930

Florence Stove Company
Gardner, Massachusetts
Stoves, 1932

Westinghouse Electric Company
East Pittsburgh, Pennsylvania
Electric Roasters, 1938

Saco Uniforms
Philadelphia, Pennsylvania
Military and Industrial Uniforms, 1948

Oroweat Baking Company
Los Angeles, California
Bread, 1937

Jantzen Knitting Mills
Portland, Oregon
Swimming Suits, 1945

American Latex Corporation
New York, New York
Bathing Caps, 1934

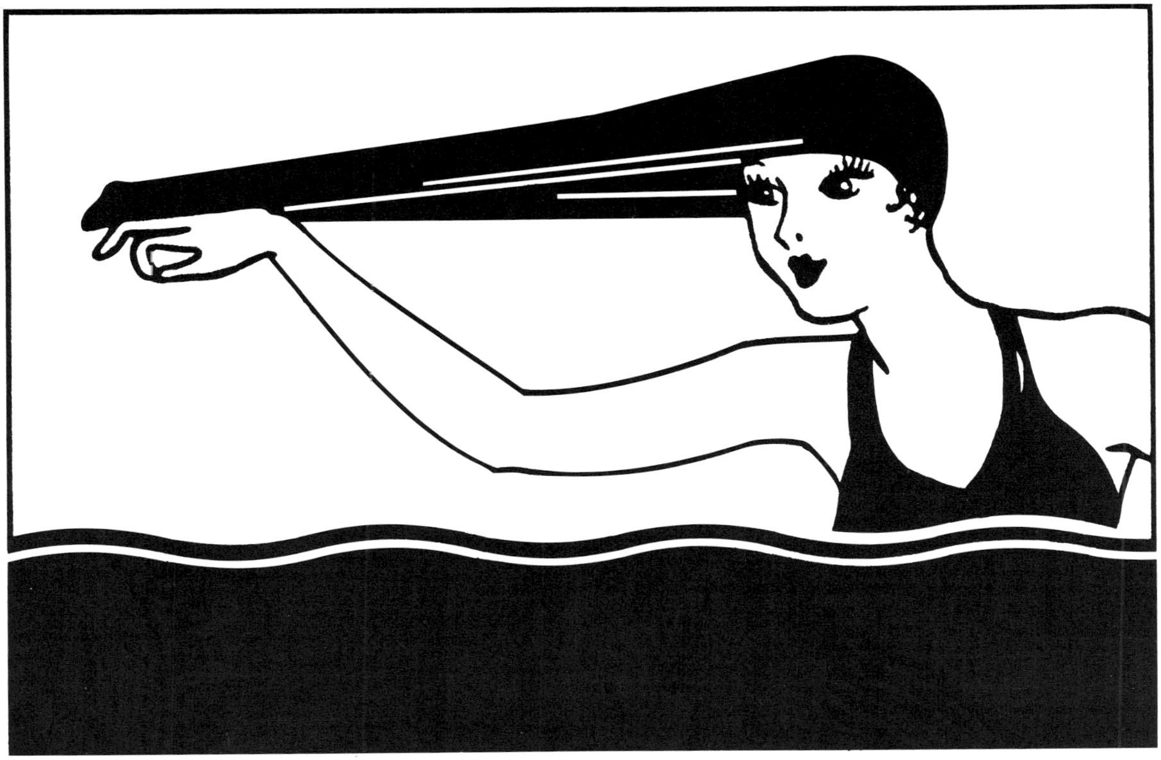

United States Rubber Company
Mishiwaka, Indiana
Foam Rubber Sponges, c. 1947

Pittsburgh Plate Glass Company
Columbia Chemical Division
Pittsburgh, Pennsylvania
Chemicals, c. 1937

The Hygenic Products Company
Canton, Ohio
Cleaning Powder for Water-Closet Bowls, 1938

No Mend Hosiery, Incorporated
Philadelphia, Pennsylvania
Hosiery, 1939

Sun-Maid Raisin Growers of California
Fresno, California
Raisin Bread, 1935

Continental Undergarment Company
Brooklyn, New York
Ladies' Underwear, 1937

Famous Products Company
Chicago, Illinois
Pharmaceutical Preparations, 1939

Bulova Watch Company
New York, New York
Watches, 1947

Plomb Tool Company
Los Angeles, California
Hexagon Power Sockets, c.1948

Antoine de Paris, Incorporated
New York, New York
Cosmetics, 1932

Mitchell Brothers Incorporated
New York, New York
Women's Underwear, 1940

Peters and Russell, Incorporated
Springfield, Ohio
Automobile Accessories, 1936

Cinamette Corporation
New York, New York
Motion Picture Cameras, 1930

SEALED
POWER
PISTON
RINGS

The Modern Library
New York, New York
Book Publishing, c.1930

Richard Hudnut
New York, New York
Cosmetics, c.1935

Pittsburgh Glass Institute
Pittsburgh, Pennsylvania
Competition Service Mark, 1937

Yeomans Brothers Company
Chicago, Illinois
Pumping Machinery, c.1935

Mullins Manufacturing Corporation
New York, New York
Pressed Metal Parts, c.1937

Art Academy of Cincinnati
Cincinnati, Ohio
193[illegible]

Summerbell Roof Structures
Los Angeles, California
Construction Materials, c. 1947

The American Tobacco Company
New York, New York
Cigarettes, 1935

Waukesha Roxo Company
Milwaukee, Wisconsin
Soft Drinks and Mixers, 1934

Marine Products Company
San Diego, California
Canned Tuna, 1937

High Duke Products Company
Chicago, Illinois
Hair Dressing and Shampoo, 1939

Albert Miller & Company
Chicago, Illinois
Potatoes, 1938

H.J. Heinz Company
Pittsburgh, Pennsylvania
Tomato Juice, 1937

The Merrill Packing Company
Salinas, California
Fresh Vegetables, 1934

Lemon-Up Company
New Orleans, Louisiana
Soft Drink, 1937

Bu-Tay Products, Incorporated
Huntington Park, California
Washing, Bluing, and Water Softener, 1941

Philadelphia Quartz Company
Philadelphia, Pennsylvania
Silicate of Soda, 1937

Doughnut Corporation of America
New York, New York
Prepared Flour for Doughnuts, 1937

American Sponge & Chamois Company
New York, New York
Sponges, 1934

Orange-Crush Company
Chicago, Illinois
Soft Drinks, 1946

Kellogg Company
Battle Creek, Michigan
Cereal Breakfast Foods, 1941

E.C. Ortega Company
Los Angeles, California
Tomato and Green Chili Juice, 1940

Detective Comics, Incorporated
New York, New York
Superman, 1941

Piggly Wiggly Corporation
Jacksonville, Florida
Food Products, 1947

Detective Comics, Incorporated
New York, New York
The Batman, 1939

Joe Lowe Corporation
New York, New York
Toys, 1939

Reddy Kilowatt
194[illegible]

REDDY KILOWATT

The Mighty Atom

Reddy Kilowatt
Service Marks, 1943-1950

Duro-Test Corporation
North Bergen, New Jersey
Fluorescent Lamps, 1945

The Hotel Stevens
Chicago, Illinois
1930

Permanente Cement Company
Oakland, California
Cement, 1944

Artstone Rocor Corporation
Brooklyn, New York
Cement Stucco, c.1935

Code Manufacturing Corporation
Coraopolis, Pennsylvania
Carbon Paper, 1942

New York - Phoenix School of Design
New York, New York
c.1945

The Mark Hopkins & Fairmont Hotels
San Francisco, California
c.1934

A.H. Geuting Company
Philadelphia, Pennsylvania
Shoes, 1932

Upjohn Company
New York, New York
Pharmaceuticals, 1943

Intertype
Brooklyn, New York
Typesetting Service Mark, 1947

Medford and Martin Hotels
Milwaukee, Wisconsin
Service Mark, 1936

Levy Bros. & Adler Rochester
Rochester, New York
Men's and Boys' Suits, 1937

Levy Bros. & Adler Rochester
Rochester, New York
Men's and Boys' Suits, 1938

Container Service Company
Reading, Pennsylvania
Shipping Containers, 1936

Tennessee Valley Authority
Electric Power, 1933

Southern California Gas Company
Los Angeles, California
c.1930

American District Steam Company
North Tonawanda, New York
Utility, c.1935

McGraw Edison Company
Chicago, Illinois
Power Transmission Equipment, c.1947

Thomas A. Edison, Incorporated
West Orange, New Jersey
Utility, c.1940

Green's Fuel, Incorporated
Sarasota, Florida
Gas Storage Tanks, 1939

Gas Company and Gas Appliance Dealers
Service Mark, 1939

Gas Company and Gas Appliance Dealers
Service Marks, c. 1937, 1943

Pacific Coast Gas Association
San Francisco, California
Service Mark, 1933

Usco Power Equipment Corporation
Birmingham, Alabama
Electrical Equipment, 1948

Universal Cooler Corporation
Detroit, Michigan
Air Conditioners, 1930

Hoskins Manufacturing Company
Detroit, Michigan
Nickel-Chromium Alloys, c.1940

United Shoes Machinery Corporation
Boston, Massachusetts
Shoe Manufacturing Equipment, 1941

Edward A. Brass
Shreveport, Louisiana
Fire Alarms, 1943

Belle City Malleable Iron Company
Racine, Wisconsin
Metal Castings, 1933

Frito New York, Incorporated
Mamaroneck, New York
Potato Chips, 1950

Sporting Goods, Incorporated
Springfield, Massachusetts
Golf Clubs and Golf Balls, 1946

Reuland Electric Company
Alhambra, California
Electric Motors, c.1948

Rayox Sales Company
Cleveland, Ohio
Water Softener, 1939

Special Chemicals Corporation
New York, New York
Plating Chemicals, 1942

Len-Pep Company
Allentown, Pennsylvania
Lubricating Oils, 1932

Indianapolis Glove Company
Indianapolis, Indiana
Work Gloves, 1947

Edwards and Company
Norwalk, Connecticut
Electric Signaling Equipment, c.1942

Indianapolis Glove Company
Indianapolis, Indiana
Work Gloves, 1947

Aerovox Corporation
New Bedford, Massachusetts
Electrolytic Condensers, 1947

Stearns Magnetic Manufacturing Company
Milwaukee, Wisconsin
Magnetic Pulleys and Drums, c. 1946

Federal Steel Sash Company
Waukesha, Wisconsin
Electric Arc Welders, c. 1935

Littleford Brothers, Incorporated
Cincinnati, Ohio
Welding Equipment, c. 1935

Downingtown Iron Works
Downingtown, Pennsylvania
Heat Exchangers, c. 1948

Apollo Manufacturing Company
Rialto, California
Fireworks, c.1947

Northern Pacific Railway
St. Paul, Minnesota
c. 1942

Royal Gorge Route
c. 1935

Union Pacific System
1930

National Mediation Board
United States Government
1934

Association of American Railroads
Washington D.C.
1943

Burlington Route
Chicago, Illinois
1934

Missouri Pacific Lines
St. Louis, Missouri
1930

Association of American Railroads
Washington, D.C.
1943

Office of Civilian Defense
Washington, D.C.
Insignia, 1942

Army Air Force
United States Government
1947

Office of Defense Transportation
United States Government
1942

Women War Workers
Washington D.C.
1943

Employment Service
United States Government
1943

Third War Loan
United States Government
1943

War Production Board
United States Government
1943

Sixth War Loan
United States Government
1944

Sixth War Loan
United States Government
1944

Health and Welfare Services
United States Government
1942

U.S. Food Emblem
Department of Agriculture
Design: Walt Disney, 1942

Department of Agriculture
United States Government
Design: Clarence Hornung, 1942

Campbell Soup Company
Camden, New Jersey
1943

Victory Symbol
1943

The Van Dorn Iron Works Company
Cleveland, Ohio
Armor Plate, c.1944

Better Vision Institute
New York, New York
Victory Symbol, 1942

VISION FOR VICTORY

Vancoram
New York, New York
Metals, c. 1947

METALS VANCORAM ALLOYS

Atlas Powder Company
Wilmington, Delaware
Industrial Explosives, c.1940

Pemco Corporation
Baltimore, Maryland
Chemicals, c.1944

Fuller Transmissions, Incorporated
New York, New York
Automobile Transmissions, c.1947

Joseph Schlitz Brewing Company
Milwaukee, Wisconsin
Beer, 1939

Erpi Classroom Films, Incorporated
New York, New York
Educational Films, c.1940

Chilean Nitrate Educational Bureau
Los Angeles, California
Nitrate of Soda, 1937

All-American Insurance Company
Washington, D.C.
Insurance, 1948

Mor-Sun Company
New York, New York
Furnaces, c.1948

Globe-Union Incorporated
New York, New York
Industrial Equipment, c.1947

Planet Manufacturing Corporation
Bloomfield, New Jersey
Electrical Capacitors, 1949

Ringling Bros. - Barnum & Bailey Combined Shows
Sarasota, Florida
Circus Entertainment, 1933

Reichhold Chemicals, Incorporated
Detroit, Michigan
Resins, 1939

Socialist Workers Party
1938

Toastmasters International
Santa Ana, California
Training in Public Speaking, 1949

Time, Incorporated
New York, New York
Weekly Magazine, 1950

National Aircraft Show
Detroit, Michigan
Service Mark, 1931

National Air Travel Week
Service Mark, 1938

Los Angeles County Fair
Pomona, California
1939

A Century of Progress
Chicago, Illinois
Service Mark, 1933

Dr. A. Posner Shoes, Incorporated
New York, New York
Shoes, 1944

Good Luck Glove Company
Carbondale, Illinois
Work Gloves, 1947

The New York Air Brake Company
Watertown, New York
Hydraulic Pumps, 1943

Skyway Luggage Company
Seattle, Washington
Luggage, 1947

Houghton Mifflin Company
New York, New York
Textbook Service Mark, 1943

Autoflight Instruments
Pasadena, California
Aircraft Controls, c.1946

United Airlines
Chicago, Illinois
c.1937

Bendix Brake Company
South Bend, Indiana
Aircraft Brakes, c.1935

Pan American Airlines
New York, New York
1944

Northrop Corporation
Los Angeles, California
Aircraft, c. 1947

Wisconsin Central Airlines
Milwaukee, Wisconsin
Design: Karl Brocken, c. 1947

Delta Airlines
Atlanta, Georgia
c. 1930

Chevron
San Francisco, California
Airplane Gasoline, c. 1937

Red-Bar Battery Company
Dayton, Ohio
Storage Batteries, 1936

Visible Index Corporation
Long Island City, New York
Duplicating Apparatus, 1949

The Huffman Manufacturing Company
Dayton, Ohio
Bicycles, 1948

National Safety Council
New York, New York
c. 1935

The Waco Aircraft Company
Troy, Ohio
Aircraft, c. 1935

L.J. Wing Manufacturing Company
New York, New York
Aircraft, c. 1930

Chance Vought Corporation
Los Angeles, California
Aircraft, c. 1940

The Globe Machine & Stamping Company
Cleveland, Ohio
Service Mark, 1943

Americar-Willys
Detroit, Michigan
Vehicles, 1940

Crouse-Hinds Company
Syracuse, New York
Airport Controls, 1946

Richfield Oil Company
Houston, Texas
Design: Clarence Hornung, c. 1947

Federal Ball Bearings Company
Poughkeepsie, New York
Ball Bearings, c. 1947

Consolidated Aircraft Corporation
San Diego, California
Aircraft, c. 1945

Marchant Calculating Machine Company
Oakland, California
Calculating Machines, 1948

Coca-Cola Company
Atlanta, Georgia
Soft Drink, c.1944

Republic Steel Corporation
Cleveland, Ohio
Steel Products, 1943

Appalachian Hardwood Manufacturers
Cincinnati, Ohio
Hardwoods, c.1935

War Assets Administration
United States Government
1946

Whitney Museum of American Art
New York, New York
c. 1942

National Gallery of Art
Washington, D.C.
1947

Fairview Colleries Corporation
Indianapolis, Indiana
Coal, 1942

FLAMINGO
WASHED COAL
Fulton Co. Ill.

Lydia V. Billing
Piedmont, California
Hair Grower, 1936

Lawrence Paper Company
Lawrence, Kansas
Paper Boxes, 1935

Riverton Lime Company
Riverton, Virginia
Cement and Lime Mixtures, 1930

Sarra Incorporated
New York, New York
Commercial Photography, c.1949

The Karpark Corporation
Cincinnati, Ohio
Parking Meters, c. 1945

Certain-teed Products Corporation
New York, New York
Beaver Board Service Mark, c. 1935

American Potash & Chemical Company
New York, New York
Borax Service Mark, c. 1930

Bear Manufacturing Company
Rock Island, Illinois
Wheel Alignment Equipment, c. 1945

Mutual Oil Company, Incorporated
Birmingham, Alabama
Gasoline, 1940

Fidalgo Island Packing Company
Seattle, Washington
Canned Salmon, 1931

Golden Bear Cookie Company
Long Island City, New York
Cookies, 1930

Edo Aircraft Corporation
Long Island, New York
Aircraft, c.1937

John C. Stuver
Barberton, Ohio
Coal, 1937

Oroville-Cordell Fruit Growers
Oroville, Washington
Fresh Apples, 1935

King Novelty Company
Chicago, Illinois
Candles, 1940

Valley Forge Envelopes & Paper Company
Philadelphia, Pennsylvania
Paper for Carbon Sheets, 1935

Spratt's Patent Limited
Newark, New Jersey
Dog Biscuits, 1938

Barker Products
Montclair, New Jersey
Dog Treatments, 1935

Walter G. Legge
New York, New York
Dog Shampoo, 1935

The Greyhound Lines
San Francisco, California
Bus Transportation, 1937

Ross Operating Valve Company
Detroit, Michigan
Air Control Valves, c.1940

The Johnston-Shelton Company
Dayton, Ohio
Clothing, 1940

Hat Corporation of America
Norwalk, Connecticut
Hats, 1935

Cannon Shoe Company
Baltimore, Maryland
Shoes, 1945

The Western Lithograph Company
Wichita, Kansas
Commercial Printing, 1949

Hart Schaffner & Marx
Chicago, Illinois
Men's Clothing, 1948

Murphy Varnish Company
Newark, New Jersey
Varnishes and Enamels, c.1935

I.C. Isaacs & Company
Baltimore, Maryland
Riding Breeches and Coats, 1935

TRADE SYMBOL

American Woolen Company
New York, New York
Knitting Yarns, c.1937

The Hartford
Hartford, Connecticut
Insurance, 1930

Natura, Incorporated
Seattle, Washington
Cosmetics, 1933

California Spray-Chemical Company
Berkeley, California
Pest Control, 1930

ANT·B·GON
KILLS ANTS

The Walter T. Kelley Company
Paducah, Kentucky
Bees, 1939

Jacques G. Golderer
New York, New York
Flypaper, 1932

Watson Manufacturing Company
Jamestown, New York
Window Screens, c.1935

Shell Oil Company
Shell Entomology
San Francisco, California
Pesticide Service Mark, 1938

General Motors Corporation
Detroit, Michigan
Service Mark, c. 1937

Contractors Machinery Company
Batavia, New York
Road Construction Machinery, 1930

Santa Fe Trailways
Chicago, Illinois
Bus Transportation, c. 1940

Ford Motor Company
Dearborn, Michigan
Service Mark, c. 1935

Trico Products Corporation
Buffalo, New York
Windshield Wipers, 1947

AC Spark Plug Division
General Motors Corporation
Detroit, Michigan
Spark Plugs, c.1940

Standard of California
Los Angeles, California
Gasoline, c.1942

BG Spark Plugs
New York, New York
c.1938

John Johnson Flooring Company
Los Angeles, California
Hardwood Flooring, c. 1934

American Potash and Chemical Company
New York, New York
c. 1939

Aluminum Corporation of America
New York, New York
Aluminum, c. 1930

Firecraft Door Company
Chicago, Illinois
Fire Doors, c. 1935

Better Homes and Gardens
Des Moines, Iowa
Magazine Service Mark, c.1947

Westinghouse Electric Company
Westinghouse Electronics Division
East Pittsburgh, Pennsylvania
Electronic Equipment, c.1947

Media Records, Incorporated
New York, New York
Business Records and Bulletins, 1930

The J.B. Ford Company
Wyandotte, Michigan
Service Mark, 1937

Pittsburgh Plate Glass Company
Paint Division
Pittsburgh, Pennsylvania
Sun-Proof Paints, 1937

The Craftex Company
Boston, Massachusetts
Paint, c.1930

Sunkist Oranges
San Joaquin Valley, California
c.1935

Globe "Al" Products
San Francisco, California
Flour, c.1935

Berks-Lehigh Cooperative Fruit Growers
Boyertown, Pennsylvania
Apple Juice, 1940

Dole Pineapple
Honolulu, Hawaii
Design: A.M. Cassandre, c.1947

Medomak Canning Company
Rockland, Maine
Canned Squash and Pumpkin, 1935

Minnesota Valley Canning Company
Le Sueur, Minnesota
Canned Corn, 1943

The Mountain Copper Company
San Francisco, California
Chemicals, 1941

Buckeye Brass and Manufacturing Company
Cleveland, Ohio
Hardware, c.1935

Gravymaster Company
Long Island City, New York
Vegetable Seasoning, 1947

Mary Chess, Incorporated
New York, New York
Toilet Preparations, 1932

The American Registry of X-Ray Technicians
Minneapolis, Minnesota
1934

F.E. Myers & Brothers Company
Ashland, Ohio
Plumbing Equipment, c.1947

The Coleman Lamp and Stove Company
Wichita, Kansas
Gas Stoves, c.1935

National Carbon Company
New York, New York
Graphite Electrodes, 1948

Butler Paper Company
Chicago, Illinois
Bond Papers, 1936

Better Housing Program
Washington, D.C.
c 1947

National Powder Extinguisher Corporation
Jersey City, New Jersey
Fire Extinguishers, 1941

International Bank
Washington, D.C.
Banking Periodicals, 1947

Boy Scouts of America
Dallas, Texas
1941

D.W. Haering & Company
Chicago, Illinois
Organic Glucosates, c.1948

Wayside Gardens
Mentor, Ohio
Nursery Supplies, c.1935

Thompson Products, Incorporated
Cleveland Ohio
Building Products, c.1939

A.M. Castle & Company
Chicago, Illinois
Construction Materials, 1939

The Globe Company
Chicago, Illinois
Meat-Packing Equipment, c.1947

Central National Bank of Cleveland
Cleveland, Ohio
Service Mark, 1947

The Jeffrey Manufacturing Company
Columbus, Ohio
Steel Mill Chains, c.1937

American Labor Party
1937

Continental Steel Corporation
Kokomo, Indiana
Steel Products Service Mark, c. 1937

Heinemann Electric Company
Trenton, New Jersey
Circuit Breakers, 1949

American Chain Link Fence Company
Medford, Massachusetts
Chain Link Fences, c. 1935

The Geometric Tool Company
New Haven, Connecticut
Taps and Dies, 1948

Arthur Glass
New York, New York
Cutlery, 1947

American Electronics, Incorporated
Los Angeles, California
Electronic Recording Equipment, 1949

Diamant Typographic Service
New York, New York
Typography, c.1948

Precision Automotive Components Company
St. Louis, Missouri
Automotive Machinery, 1946

Robert Gair, Incorporated
New York, New York
Paperboard Cartons, c.1947

Anchor Hocking Glass Corporation
Lancaster, Ohio
Glass Bottles, 1938

O.B. Andrews Company
New York, New York
Paper Cartons, c.1947

Chicago Eye Shield Company
Chicago, Illinois
Eye Protection, c.1947

Columbia Broadcasting System
New York, New York
Radio Broadcasting, 1950
Design: William Golden

Columbia Broadcasting System
New York, New York
Phonograph Records, 1939

Otis Elevator Company
Jersey City, New Jersey
Elevators, 1937

Trane
LaCrosse, Wisconsin
Climate Control Machinery, c.1945

The Charles Breneman Company
Cincinnati, Ohio
Window Shades, 1946

Electro-Protective Corporation
Newark, New Jersey
Fire and Burglar Alarms, 1938

Old Colony Furniture Company
New York, New York
Furniture, c.1940

The Scholl Manufacturing Company
Chicago, Illinois
Arch Supports, 1948

Bigelow-Sanford Carpet Company
New York, New York
Carpets, c.1930

Denison Engineering Company
Columbus, Ohio
Industrial Equipment, c.1945

The Powers Regulator Company
Chicago, Illinois
Temperature Controllers, c.1948

Glyco Products Company
New York, New York
Chemical Compounds, 1935

Advertising Agencies' Service Company
New York, New York
Typography, c. 1947

American Type Founders
Elizabeth, New Jersey
Service Marks, 1937

Acme Steel Company
Chicago, Illinois
Doc Steelstrap, c.1937

The National Screw & Manufacturing Company
Cleveland, Ohio
Screws and Bolts, 1945

The Sisalkraft Company
Chicago, Illinois
Insulation, c.1948

USL Battery Corporation
Niagara Falls, New York
Industrial Batteries, c.1937

National Biscuit Company
New York, New York
Biscuits, c. 1930

Allis-Chalmers Corporation
Milwaukee, Wisconsin
Industrial Equipment, c. 1940

Sundstrand Machine Tool Company
Rockford, Illinois
Lathes, c. 1944

The Resinous Products & Chemical Company
Philadelphia, Pennsylvania
Glue Film, c. 1935

Johns-Manville
New York, New York
Insulation, c. 1930

Ballantine Laboratories, Incorporated
Boonton, New Jersey
Electronic Voltmeters, c. 1946

Addressograph-Multigraph Corporation
Cleveland, Ohio
Lithographic Plates, 1931

Magnaflux Corporation
Chicago, Illinois
Industrial Equipment, c. 1947

The Korfund Company
Long Island City, New York
Soundproofing, c. 1935

Universal Gypsum & Lime Company
Chicago, Illinois
Gypsum and Lime Products, c. 1930

The Garrett Corporation
Los Angeles, California
Air Conditioners, 1940

H.E. Fletcher Company
West Chelmsford, Massachusetts
Granite, c. 1935

Sterling Engraving Company
New York, New York
Photoengraving, c. 1945

Hafner Fabrics
New York, New York
Fabrics, c. 1944

Armour and Company
Chicago, Illinois
Pharmaceuticals, 1949

The First National Bank of Chicago
Chicago, Illinois
Commercial Savings, 1947

Detroit Show Case Company
Detroit, Michigan
Store Fronts, c.1935

Lisle Corporation
Clarinda, Iowa
Tools, c.1948

Phelan-Faust Paint Company
St. Louis, Missouri
Enamel Paint, 1936

Anna Maria Wilkins
Mobile, Alabama
Soft Drinks, 1938

Nedlick's Stores, Incorporated
New York, New York
Soft Drinks, 1945

Mundet Cork Corporation
New York, New York
Cork Products, c.1935

Fosko

Nesbitt's

Jointite
TRADE MARK

The Aro Equipment Corporation
Bryan, Ohio
Industrial Lubricating Equipment, 1937

Sugs, Incorporated
Belleville, Illinois
Sugar-Coated Nuts, 1939

Swank, Incorporated
New York, New York
Jewelry, c. 1940

Elgin Watch Company
Elgin, Illinois
Watches, c. 1940

Garrett Supply Company
Los Angeles, California
Industrial Supplies, c. 1935

SWANK

ELGIN

GARRETT
SUPPLY COMPANY

Rockwell-Barnes Company
Chicago, Illinois
Stenographic Notebooks, 1935

EASEL

John Francis Briskey
Birmingham, Alabama
Trading Stamps, 1948

The Newport Company
Carrollville, Wisconsin
Turpentine, 1930

Motorola Incorporated
Chicago, Illinois
Radio and Television Sets, c.1947
Design: J.O. Reinecke and Associates

Corning Glass Works
Corning, New York
Glassware, 1947

Delta-Star Electric Company
Chicago, Illinois
Electrical Equipment, 1947

New Deal
1936

Orefraction Incorporated
Pittsburgh, Pennsylvania
Ceramic Materials, 1941

Atomic Energy Commission
United States Government
c. 1949

Cleveland Institute of Art
Cleveland, Ohio
19[illegible]9

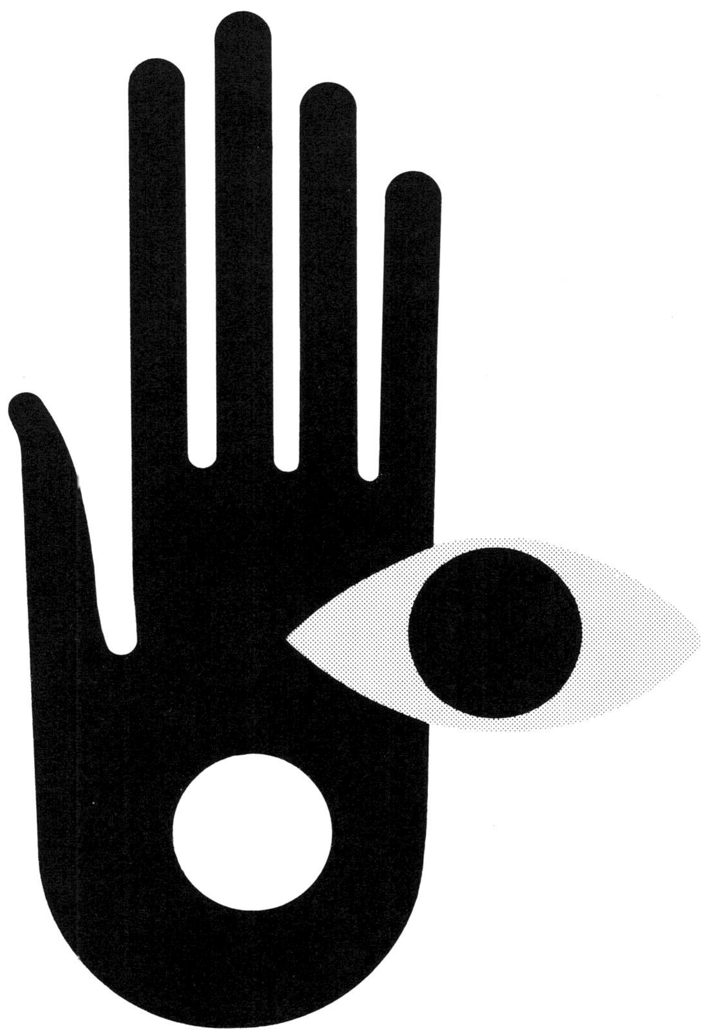